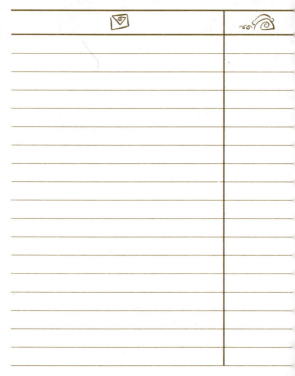

D

D

D

E

F

F

J
K

✉	🐚

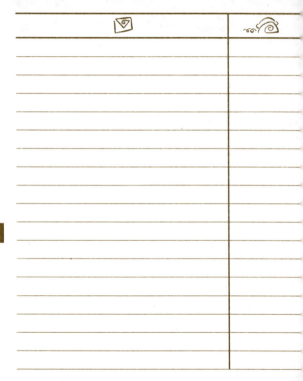

P

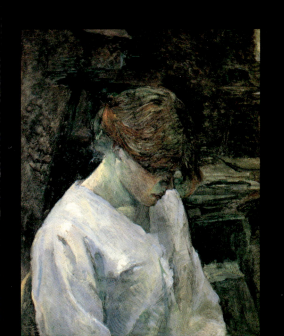

S

S

S

Thomas, Julia & Peter
Altyre House
Gordonstoun School
Elgin, Moray
IV30 5RB
(01343) 837 852
ptthomas@dircon.co.uk

T

U

U

U

XYZ

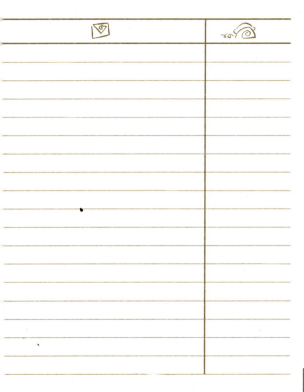

Camille Pissarro
La calle Saint-Honoré después
del mediodía. Efecto de lluvia, 1897
The Street Saint-Honoré after Midday. Effects of Rain
Die Strasse Saint-Honoré am Nachmittag bei Regen
Museo Thyssen-Bornemisza, Madrid

A
Camille Pissarro
La calle Saint-Honoré después
del mediodía. Efecto de lluvia, 1897
The Street Saint-Honoré after Midday. Effects of Rain
Die Strasse Saint-Honoré am Nachmittag bei Regen
Museo Thyssen-Bornemisza, Madrid

B
Camille Pissarro
La calle Saint-Honoré después
del mediodía. Efecto de lluvia, 1897, detalle
The Street Saint-Honoré after Midday. Effects of Rain, detail
Die Strasse Saint-Honoré am Nachmittag bei Regen, Detail
Museo Thyssen-Bornemisza, Madrid

C - CH
Camille Pissarro
El bosque de Marly, 1871
The Marly Forest
Der Wald von Marly

Museo Thyssen-Bornemisza, Madrid

D
Camille Pissarro
El bosque de Marly, 1871, detalle
The Marly Forest, detail
Der Wald von Marly, Detail

Museo Thyssen-Bornemisza, Madrid

E
Berthe Morisot
El espejo de vestir, 1876
The Dressing Mirror
Der Ankleidespiegel

Museo Thyssen-Bornemisza, Madrid

F
Vincent Van Gogh
"Les Vessenots" en Auvers, 1890
"Les Vessenots" in Auvers
"Les Vessenots" in Auvers

Museo Thyssen-Bornemisza, Madrid

G
Vincent Van Gogh
"Les Vessenots" en Auvers, 1890, detalle
"Les Vessenots" in Auvers, detail
"Les Vessenots" in Auvers, Detail

Museo Thyssen-Bornemisza, Madrid

H - I
Vincent Van Gogh
Los descargadores en Arles, 1888
The Unloaders in Arles
Hafenarbeiter in Arles

Museo Thyssen-Bornemisza, Madrid

J - K
Edgar Degas
Bailarina basculando (Bailarina verde), 1877-79
The Swinging Ballerina (Green Ballerina)
Tänzerin, balancierend (Grüne Tänzerin)

Museo Thyssen-Bornemisza, Madrid

L - LL
Edgar Degas
Bailarina basculando (Bailarina verde), 1877-79, detalle
The Swinging Ballerina (Green Ballerina), detail
Tänzerin, balancierend (Grüne Tänzerin), Detail

Museo Thyssen-Bornemisza, Madrid

M
Edgar Degas
En la sombrerería, c. 1883
In the Hat Shop
Im Hutladen

Museo Thyssen-Bornemisza, Madrid

N
Edgar Degas
En la sombrerería, c. 1883, detalle
In the Hat Shop, detail
Im Hutladen, Detail

Museo Thyssen-Bornemisza, Madrid

O
Paul Cézanne
Retrato de un campesino, 1901-06
Portrait of a Peasant
Porträt eines Bauern

Museo Thyssen-Bornemisza, Madrid

P
Paul Cézanne
Retrato de un campesino, 1901-06, detalle
Portrait of a Peasant, detail
Porträt eines Bauern, Detail

Museo Thyssen-Bornemisza, Madrid

Q - R
Paul Cézanne
Botella, garrafa, jarro y limones, 1902-06
Bottle, Demijohn, Jar and Lemons
Flasche, Karaffe, Krug und Zitronen

Museo Thyssen-Bornemisza, Madrid

S
Henri de Toulouse-Lautrec
La pelirroja con blusa blanca, 1889
The Redhead with White Blouse
Rothaarige mit weisser Bluse

Museo Thyssen-Bornemisza, Madrid

T
Henri de Toulouse-Lautrec
Yvette Guilbert, 1893
Yvette Guilbert
Yvette Guilbert

Museo Thyssen-Bornemisza, Madrid

U
Paul Gauguin
Hombre en la carretera (Rouen), 1884
Man in the Road (Rouen)
Mann auf der Strasse (Rouen)

Museo Thyssen-Bornemisza, Madrid

V - W
Paul Gauguin
Hombre en la carretera (Rouen), 1884, detalle
Man in the Road (Rouen), detail
Mann auf der Strasse (Rouen), Detail

Museo Thyssen-Bornemisza, Madrid

X - Y - Z
Edouard Manet
Amazona de frente, c. 1882
Amazon from the Front
Reiterin von vorne

Museo Thyssen-Bornemisza, Madrid

Diseño y dirección de arte:
Estudi Viola